For

wif

*Patrick O'Connell*

MW01253249

# Hoping for Angels

# HOPING
## FOR
# ANGELS

# PATRICK
# O'CONNELL

TURNSTONE PRESS

Turnstone Press
607-100 Arthur Street
Winnipeg, Manitoba
Canada   R3B 1H3

This book was published with the assistance of the
Manitoba Arts Council and the Canada Council.

Cover design: Kelly Fraser Design

Front cover photograph by Patrick O'Connell

Back cover photograph by Sandy Brown

This book was printed and bound in Canada by
Kromar Printing Limited.

All the poems in this book were written in Winnipeg
between October 1985 and May 1990.

Canadian Cataloguing in Publication Data

O'Connell, Patrick, 1944-

Hoping for angels

Poems.
ISBN 0-88801-151-2

I. Title.

PS8579.C655H6 1990     C811/.54     C90-097125-8
PR9199.3.O365H6 1990

# Acknowledgements

The author gratefully acknowledges a
Writer's B Grant from the Manitoba Arts Council.

Some of these poems have appeared in *Quarry,*
*Prairie Fire* and *The Antigonish Review.*

Special thanks to Charles Wilkins
and David Arnason.

For Elaine Fleury

One does not become enlightened
by imagining figures of light
but by making the darkness conscious.

— C.G. Jung

# Contents

## The Blue Man Is Drowning Again

## Hoping for Angels

A Memory of Winter

## A Thousand Swallows

# THE BLUE MAN IS DROWNING AGAIN

I am Judas
on holiday from hell
                    he wailed
under the wave drench

— David Helwig

## THE BLUE MAN EXITS

sun up in flames
heaving black smoke
the carnivorous carnival
goes on
though most of them
are sleeping
their phosphorescent skin
their blue tattoos
their sighs
like molten glass
as i motor west
my road in a rear view mirror
an unbroken sequence
of white line flowing
straight into cobalt
green sky

## THE BLUE MAN'S SLATTERN

yes i loved it
when you came
opening the door
putting your lips
on my shoulder
then your gun
in my drawer
your fierce brilliant
mouth and eyes
so strong
even your broken teeth
looked fine
like a yellow leaf
you leaned against
the glass
crying
all the gods are broken
all the gods are broken
you cried

## THE BLUE MAN WINS A PRIZE

you who contrive to be
nothing
succeed
and win
a bottle of cheap brandy
and a cardboard hat
yodelling out the caboose window
as the train wheels
hum the track
any day now
an abyss will crack
opening
under your crazy feet
already in a snowy street
a small boy is running
with flowers

## THE BLUE MAN'S LANDLORD

the old landlord
sweeping past my door
in his bare feet
he is always in his bare feet
which makes me
slightly seasick
he came one day
to fix my toilet
in his bare feet

## THE BLUE MAN'S BLITZ

if i told you
i used to burn
ants
on the sidewalk
with a magnifying
glass
you'd think
i was lying but
i still remember
the blue smoke

i even rigged up
a small gallows
i called
hang hopper hill
and hanged
grasshoppers
by white thread
this is it baby
this is the last
goddamn jump
you'll ever make
i always quoted
the bible though
before i hanged them

## THE BLUE MAN'S COMPASSIONATE NIGHT

i skip my stones
across the iron water
bang    bong
the old trees
reaching for the sky
just like november

## THE BLUE MAN WANDERS

i am a man
fire walking
boldly
up a wall

this is my vision
a brick wall
in black and white
which i ascend

thus it happens
the old apparition
of deliverance

## THE BLUE MAN'S BOOZE

two days before the detox
i was dying of loneliness
i was in a park
a man was kissing a little baby
the singers were singing
life could be a dream
sweet heart

## THE BLUE MAN IS DROWNING AGAIN

goddamn it
he says

drowning
is seeing a movie
in black and blue

he sees mouth

    snow

    blood

    chain

    fire

## THE BLUE MAN TALKS

the moon is the sum
of all my sorrow
becoming more distended
night by night

the moon is a ball
of all my old band-aids

## THE BLUE MAN GETS A PHONE CALL

X shot himself
in a phone booth
had the phone
on one ear
a gun on
the other
right in the middle
of the conversation
he said

listen to this

## THE BLUE MAN FALLS INTO OBLIVION

twilight descends
like blue dust
after a collision
and all the birds fly
flat out
as one silver wheel cover
wobbles its way
down the road
and flops with a clank

soon
you will not fear
the tramps
they are preparing
their old hats
their broken hands
are ready now
to salute you

## THE BLUE MAN HALLUCINATES

you desolate as
these stubble fields
of a wrecked season

or this smashed
windshield
of an old truck

as now a blackbird
lights upon
your shoulder

and your cry
hard
as the driving rain

there is only this road
these railway tracks
you say

# HOPING FOR ANGELS

In the deserts of the heart
let the healing fountain start

— W.H. Auden

## A FLAMING ROSE IS THROWN

Here where the water breaks
the sky
into diamonds
I open myself    I surrender
for isn't this what it all was
a preparation for love
or dying
a walk across fields
with wild grass in my hand
startling a crane into air
how under each stone
blue sky burns
for the earth is paper thin
as blossoms off a branch blow
on to the land
see the flame dance
the moonrise on the hill
unearthly flowers
white as paradise, are opening

# SEE HOW THE STARWHEEL TURNS

How each angry arm
in my mind
unfurled to a leaf
when I found the face I had
before the world
was born
walking over bridges
as the rain forms
circles on the river
patterns to be learned
for everything returns
to itself
like skylarks
or a man juggling an orange
Enchanted as I always was
by music
I come singing
now is all the time there is
for eternity to unfold
more joy in this
than a handful of ribbons
to be skating
in ever widening circles
with the wind on your face

## WHAT EVERY VAGABOND MUST TELL YOU

Everything is on the inside
the night blue air
the longing
a prairie field
that might have been there
and my own heart
that transcends the world
like a swallow
what I could not say in words
but only mouthed
do you love this life
this feast I share
with the crescent moon
and one star seen
through tree branches
this vision is simply a matter
of control
by walking at precise angles
in the street
I can chase the moon
down chimneys

## HORSEMAN

Riding over bridges and bridges
which are empty when I look
though the river is full of leaves
and birds so high in the morning sky
they have no memory of earth
wheeling like distant stars
no song to be heard
not even the mention of trees

This then is what is given to me
this is the gift I must carry
as my mind is a mirror reflecting
everything exactly as it is

Now the long arrows I aim at the sun
see how the sun has an arrow in it
as steel hooves ring out on a bridge

## WHO COULD BE MORE WONDERFUL THAN YOU

There was this man
who had us all lying on the floor
with our eyes closed
and he talked about the sun
how we had to visualize
the sun
as if the sun were inside us
sending out
these beautiful golden rays
and if we could do this
we would become so attractive
people would come up in the street
to ask where the post office was
when they already knew

And I was trying so hard
to visualize the sun but
all I could see was the moon
the way the moon appeared
outside a bus window once
like it was racing us
shooting along over the trees
how I wrote my name
in the mist of the window
and jingled my change

## BIRDIE

Sometimes in the evening
I just sit and sip tea
and quietly commune
with my pet birdie
and watch all the tricks he performs
in the luxury of time

And neither of us ever thinks about
sex or death or freedom

So there is nothing deep about this
my birdie just preens himself
drawing each long tail feather
through his yellow beak
and I get to thinking how
lucky we are to be here

And the room gets so silent
the room gets so silent sometimes
before my birdie sings

## THERE ARE MORE THINGS IN HEAVEN AND EARTH

You know the way the sand at the beach is
under your feet in the water
the sort of ribbed pattern the sand makes
well I saw the same pattern in the clouds
and have you ever noticed
how much a cauliflower resembles a tree
it amazes me
the way all the forms repeat themselves
how you keep calling my name over and over
when I am burrowed in beside the bushes
adrift in the drift of Nature, my pockets
stuffed with autumn leaves

## THE FOUNTAIN

We crossed the slippery road
into the grocery store
with bird shit on the window
and stacks of cans of cat food
everyone in this neighbourhood
has a starving cat

And the old man
the one I come with every day
speaks to me
listen he says, never forget
that mostly it is a matter of grace

I pay for a pint of milk
and three bananas
later in the park the old man and me
with our bare feet in the fountain
counting water beetles and waiting
for night

## A VISITOR

Found your slip in my bed
dreamed
the moon was filling up with snow
woke to remember
everything I know
about leaves
lighting the stove under the kettle
to the hum of the fridge
which reassures me
about this journey I make
across rooms
as the sun slips behind clouds
my rooms darken
only now do I discover
rain is blue
and you
brushing your hair which gathers
all the light

## THE RETURN OF THE NATIVE

Eustacia the Indian girl quit it all
maybe for sure
left the city and ended
her cigar-butt Main Street days
and moved back to the reserve
where there is a rink on a river
and an old Jeep in the yard
at a Friday dance in the bingo hall
the stars will tumble across the sky
as the dark-eyed Indians reel

She came back to town once
on a Greyhound bound for Winnipeg
sat in the front seat all the way
went right to the North End Pawnshop
looked the guy in the eye
and got her mandolin out of hock

## THE COURAGE OF CLOWNS

All the years it has taken
to empty
for the hard edge of my dream
to resolve

Like the worn planks
which make a path in a garden
lilacs which shed their blossoms
months ago
wait in the August rain

All night I listened to
the thunder
for the earth is a broken bell
which rings
like a bird in an open window

Like the courage of clowns
with their wide open faces
laughing
all the way to town

Watching how the night falls
right into their arms

## A ROOM IN JUNE

Tonight it is simply enough
to breathe the fragrant air

A bird sings in my room
peace has come

Though I have not made many choices
so, in a way, I was delivered here

Into this room where
I have blown the candles out

Later, there will be dreams
to come

Last night I dreamed of horses
running, through a burning field

And you may ask
what manner of faith have I lived by

I would tell you silence
is the only word

## LOVE AND DEATH

I took three pebbles in my hands
and shook them like a rattle

Someday your bones
will sound like that

Each wave washing in
dissolving light

Drawing the earth back under
the ancient lake

Death you say is a penance
compelling us to love

As the huge sky dreams
a fish-skeleton cloud formation

The moon in the afternoon
in its eye

## MY COMPANION

The old man at 84 sits up
in his hospital bed
and writes me notes
because the man can't speak anymore
so I ask how he is feeling
and he writes me a note that says
ok
his tired thin legs
and the hollowness of him
note by note
we cover all his concerns
and finally I ask
is there anything else I can get you
and he writes
maybe you could get me a redhead
maybe you could waltz her in
open all the windows up for the moon
and let the curtains blow in

RIDING INTO THE SUNSET

Look
see how the sky
is a horse on fire

As here we are again
by a lake
blue reflections oscillate

And I can see two images
of your face

How then
shall I describe you

I never could tell
the difference between
a feather and a leaf

Now answer this question
was sex God's mistake

Yes I cried
I love a bell

So this is what it comes to
you say

Peeling another orange
as each musical fish leaps

In the air

## SILVER WIND SING THE TREE

Feeling my heart beat
its miracles
I try to explain
that the moon is oval
how I discovered
the night
in my own wings
the way birds are as men
fleeing for sky
when all that we have
is the simple task
of remembering
the forage
our own courage brings
for it is always the work
that saves us
walking down alleys
watching the old girl
hang out the wash
a cigarette on her lip
her pockets
full of clothes pegs
and sheets that billow
like great white truths
in the lane

## INNER RICHES

That was all the beauty
I could afford
in those days
shining my shoes
and seeing my own breath
in the yard
my tree full of birds
in naked celebration
just so pleased
by the colour of snow
with my eyes closed
looking within
at hidden wonders
like a man flying
on a trapeze
or a salvation more lovely
than rain
and I call it a song
I will sing for earth
and the tangled streets
that I live in
I tell you
I love my poverty
no horse ever went as far
on a bag of oats
as I did

## SOMEWHERE NEAR REGINA

How once you lay
in a wheatfield
with a long forgotten mate
on warm August earth
as waves of a gold ocean
rolled over you
somewhere near Regina

Walking free
wide rings of fire
around us
stubble fields
smoking the sky

This is a memory

A white horse
in wind-blown night field
neighing
at the turquoise moon

Later the dance hall
drinking outside in the truck
the sweet scent of burnt stubble
in her hair

## ON THE DEATH OF A FRIEND

for George Wilson (1905-1989)

When I saw my shadow
on the river from a bridge
I knew
I exist on edges
all my hands are turning
into leaves
a small knot in my throat
that is not fear
but sorrow
for the way time shatters
a man
swollen with pain
in a hospital room
with basins
lost in the blizzard
of his oblivion
I simply took his hand
and said, George
I have loved you
I have kissed the face
of the dying
and lusted after nurses
I have looked in mirrors
and seen your own face
in place of mine

## THE VISITATION

for Dylan Thomas

He told us
his glass turned
into a fish
this was his expectation
how wild the night was
when an angel appeared
to him

In a room
with a burnt out lightbulb
bare feet and
a carton of cigarettes
not to mention
the bottles

But he was never sure
thought maybe
it was the D.T.'s again
writing a poem desperately
across a page

## TRYING TO SPEAK A LANGUAGE

In dreams you speak
of ships that rise
and fall upon the ocean
last night I found a seagull
in our bed
those one night stands
in bleak dockside hotels
even in those paper rooms
I could smell the waves
I could see the sea break
in your eyes
like little navigators
with ancient scrolls
trying to chart our way across
an unmade bed
arriving at the breaking place
of reason
morning tide and foghorns
always there were foghorns
a distant warning
trying to speak a language
only a bird would understand

## EATON'S

Old women picking through a bin
of winter hats for sale
like old crows
talking into mirrors and saying
nothing
how there is always something
to be denied
the memory of 80 winters
all lined up in a row
like winter clothes pegs
on a frozen line
as the cashier
a blonde girl from Minnedosa
blows her nose
all the Christmas songs reminding me
of joy
the blue bruise of the sky
the slit in my left shoe
the drunk stuck in revolving doors
my hungry illusory self
nearing surrender

## HEAVEN IS A POINT ON A WHEEL

I am becoming a little seedy
eat once a day now out of a pot
breaking phrases in an unswept room
as the night sails blue and alone
something like the wind along
the river     still

I remember the dolls of your room
upon the dresser
I thought I could still see them
after you turned out the light

Our arms then found each other
to the sound of rain starting on trees
I didn't know then or had forgotten
heaven is a point on a wheel

# THE PHOTOGRAPH

The first snowfall this year
having my picture taken by you
out on the prairie
the curving form the plough made
on the contour of fields
everything you need to create
a mythology
the distant farm
the bullet riddled sign that reads
Texaco Gasoline
the gradual whitening of fields
the whole world abandoning itself
for a new form
standing in front of your camera
after my life burned down
I stood on the tip of one finger
eating fire

## JOY WILL FIND A WAY

In a grey March winter sky
high black branches sway
songs of a hard season
as tiny voices    echo
under a bridge
if only we could hear
God spinning his wheel
delivering our days to us
like letters under a door
twilight and evening star
rivers to cross
how night comes at me
like a thorn
like snow in June
like frost on all the garden
the trick is
to avoid your own reflection
to walk over the pieces
of the broken mirror
I tell you
Enlightenment is easy
some days all you have to do
is put your shoes on

## THE LIGHT IN THE STREAM

And once I sat in a river
by tall poplars
silver blue minnows came
to my legs
yellow leaves gathered
on my tent
the wisdom of the stream
like a mind seeking a way
around absurdity
I wander through rivers
of time
the mirage of sky tricks
on water
where all shadows merge
into the shape of a man
it is my own heart
my own wheel, I have to conquer

## SONG

My winter buckled
into ribbons
which burned
there is a sky in me
breaking open
rain speaking words
to a leaf
and something as final
as this
looking
at the shape of things
and finding myself
again
forever in the spiral
of spring

## FINAL MOMENTS

Waiting
for the room to go dark
and when it does
I will tell you everything
about twilight
how this dusk falls
like slow birds
like dark blossoms
on to my window
as my incense burns
and the music plays Chopin
thinking I could learn
whatever it is
the sky says
for only the sky knows
we are hurled into the world
like leaves
a man stripped of everything
celebrates Earth
overcomes his own ruins
like a sparrow

## SUMMER AUTUMN WINTER SPRING

To carry within
the light of the world
like a leaf on my tongue
from a garden
to genuflect in the road
to remove a stone
from one shoe
no one will ever understand
Horatio
how all the birds
on telephone wires
are like musical notes
how the thing was simply
to turn
that farmers are burning
their fields tonight
and an Indian youth
in the street
made the sound of a loon
all my taps drip in harmony
as one branch scratches
against my screen
I take this as a sign
as I go my way
seeking salvation in faces
streets doing their old dance
for rain

## HOPING FOR ANGELS

I found a long stick
with one rain drop
I wave it around in the

Sky

Each tree blowing silver
thus the world burns

See

A fire going out slowly
in the west

I, maestro
of celestial events
hoping for angels

Sing

WHAT THE MOON IS

As birds fly under bridges
to the sound of wind
in poplar trees
the cool rustle of words

Like handprints in the sand
the sea washes over
as you dream think the value

Of illusion
and mind hard as stone
you bite into
to spit the broken fragments
at the sky

Then right on the very brink
of the world
you discover
Love is round

So all you have to learn now
is a circle
how you try to write down on paper
what the moon is

## ACROBAT

I hope you can feel this
as clearly as I

That the attitude a man takes
to his own pain
determines all

Thus my flight, arched
over the hushed crowd

This is no mere exhibition
or sentiment of desire
this is where the intellect
surrenders

To vulnerability and grace

I count my hands, I spin through air

See how the light strikes
my costume

I always could see heaven
out of the corner
of one eye

## IN THIS MOONBOAT ROCKING ON THE SEA

How I came to know
faith is silence
I too know the night
is long
I have measured it
against your hem
while you were sleeping

It was night that taught me
to turn
and I turned
towards the centre
the circle was closing fast
rain rang my memory
like wind chimes
and I knew that I was saved

My heart, my solitude
how I arranged them
this way is a story
see how my hands
and my feet are bound
by a rose

# A MEMORY OF WINTER

November Separates Everything

— Paulette Jiles

## MARIE THERIAULT

So there were these 14 Stations of the Cross where you knelt and prayed at each one and finally there was a life-size Christ on his cross and you had to kneel down and kiss his nailed feet. Marie Theriault was ahead of me. She was kissing Christ's feet. And then I knelt there. I was kissing Christ's feet on the exact spot where Marie Theriault's lips had been. I was kissing Christ's feet but all I could think about was Marie Theriault.

## CREDIT CARDS

Well the job in this case was to stand just inside the door of the big department store and ask people as they came and went if they had a Bay credit card. But you have to be selective they said. We don't want any credit cards going to any bums. You can spot a bum can't you? This was the prerequisite for the job. You had to be able to spot a bum a block away.

## SURVIVAL

for Chetan Rajani

Fact is nothing much fazes me anymore. Even my
mandolin in the pawnshop window for sale for 40
bucks and me gliding by alone on a bicycle built for
two, hearing the whirr of my wheels in the rain and
a mad dog in the back of a pickup truck. One by one
the images of a world are unfolding. And O yes it
has been a hard quest for survival though recently I
have acquired the knack of disappearing into thin
air. So here I come into the glass world where
business is war and indifference is a symptom of
depression. Now you see me. Now you don't.

## THE ART OF WAITING

Here is a beautiful phrase. The Art of Waiting. Think about that for awhile. I am waiting. But to ask what I am waiting for would miss the point. I simply wait. Here is another short snapper. No man lives the life he intends. Think about the truth of that. If none of this impresses you I shall try one more. The truth moves. No wonder I could never nail it down.

## URINALS

I was pissing in a urinal alongside 5 other men but I
was never very comfortable with this kind of
arrangement. So when the guy beside me really
checked me out, that clinched it. Forever after I
pissed in the cubicles. Locked the door and hung my
grocery bag on the hook.

## SPRING OVERCOAT

I have this coat from my old days as a salesman,
London Fog trench coat, and I have dug it out and
tried it on, a little big for me now because I am
shrinking. Each year I diminish a size. So I have this
coat on and move about the room catching glimpses
of myself in the mirror as I swirl past and it looks
pretty good and you would never know to look at
me that I . . . well never mind. My life just doesn't fit
together like a German train schedule. There are
some missing parts. In a couple of places the tracks
run right into the sea. The day they landed on the
moon I was four years late for an interview, finally
arriving exhausted. They had turned the place into a
used car lot. And I am in the street now in my
London Fog trench coat and the slush is up to my
ankles and there is this pain right in the middle of
my heart and I look up and there is this 8 foot wave
of black ice water coming right at me.

## WINTERBLOOD

I never knew until tonight you could die stone cold
on a bench. I even had my picture taken in a booth.
4 little black and white photos that never arrived.
See the flame within the wind. Snow is what the
wind says when it burns. I have my own winter, my
own chaos to look into. Like a howl that turns into
silence. So a man comes up and whispers for a buck.
Some faces go on forever without being kissed.

## ICARUS

Even in the womb I dreamed flight. How a wild bird broke in my brain. The first death I came to was a season. The second death was a train horn song right on the edge of a city but by then I knew how to fly. Then the third death of which I have had a premonition. Large dark birds have me now hard in the clutch of their talons. Furiously seaward, over the Rocky Mountains.

## SISYPHUS ROLLING HIS ROCK

Thus I constantly begin. How a dark infinite
mountain begins in my mind. The worst part is there
are no others. Only the dream song of my sons
waiting like a train station clock. And blood on my
hands from the rock. To feel the bee sting of wind
and the clank and drone of my boots. In truth I have
no faith, therefore I believe in rock. The way the sky
spins. How the mountain trembles.

## I END EACH NIGHT WITH A ROSE I LIGHT, AND THROW OUT A WINDOW

I am on an escalator going up. Beside me is an escalator coming down. So up ahead I see a woman coming towards me. She has her hands in her pockets and a button is missing from her coat. And all of Time has wound its clock for this moment when we would finally meet. But the escalators are running true to themselves so there is barely time for a handshake and a kiss.

## A HOMEMADE TATTOO

I was crossing Osborne Bridge and there were an
Indian man and an Indian woman coming up from
the river bank. There were small round places in the
grass by the river where they had slept like deer. The
Indian man was rolling a cigarette and the Indian
woman was holding on to his arm. And a blonde
jogging by in $75.00 running shoes. What a laugh. I
swear I never knew the meaning of the phrase "the
freedom of the poor" until I saw the Indian kids in
the fountain.

## THE LITTLE TOWN

for Jennifer Hedges

There was a girl on a sunlit veranda. Her father was
cutting her hair. She wore a flowered skirt and sat in
a wicker chair. Their faces were so beautiful I put my
parcel down and touched my hand against a tree
and loved the little town.

## WAITING FOR THE NEXT EXPLOSION

Ruth is here. Born in Hamburg in 1943. To this day
the sound of propeller aircraft frightens her. The
Allies bombed the shit out of Hamburg. It is
November 11 today. Cannons are firing across the
town. We never could figure out if it was a 14 or a 19
gun salute. About every 30 seconds an explosion
rattles my walls and my china. Ruth and I, simply in
bed. Waiting for the next explosion.

# A THOUSAND SWALLOWS

When you overcome the earth
the stars will be yours

    — Boethius, *The Consolation
    of Philosophy*

## A WEDDING DRESS

Hazard looked in the window of the second-hand store on Princess Street. He saw an old wedding dress on a mannequin. Hazard remembered Rita then. He had rented a room in her house in 1978. Hazard once found a framed wedding picture of Rita and Ray in their attic. Rita had told him he might find the lamp he needed there. Hazard was looking at this wedding picture when noise exploded downstairs. Ray had come home drunk. He had thrown a chair through a window. Rita locked herself in the bathroom. Ray was attacking the furniture. He was tearing his whole blessed world apart. Hazard looked at the wedding dress in the second-hand store window. A building across the street was reflected in the window so what Hazard was seeing was one image superimposed on another. An old wedding dress and a black iron fire escape.

## REAL HAPPINESS

Hazard had read once that real happiness in life depended on one's ability to listen. He was standing at a red light when he remembered this. So he shut his eyes and listened. He was amazed at what he could hear.

## A TRIP TO THE SEA

Hazard had a shoe box on his closet shelf. He had
forgotten what was in it so he took it down to look.
Inside he found a small box of colour slides. Hazard
took a slide out and held it up to the light. It was a
picture of the sea. In WW II more men from the
prairies had gone to sea than maritimers. Hazard
knew that. He held another slide up to the light.
Once he had been in a small lobster boat off the coast
of Prince Edward Island. There was a thick fog and
large black swells on the sea that day. Hazard had
sat in the stern of the boat looking out into the fog.
He grew philosophical about this scene; the black
water, the fog, the Nothingness. Then the white bird
appeared out of nowhere. It landed on the black
water 10 feet off the stern. Hazard had never seen
anything so white. He started to view the world then
in terms of transformations.

## A BIG ONE

Hazard had wanted to catch a big fish in those days
so he hired Thomas. Thomas had been written up in
*Field and Stream* in 1957 and had become so bushed
once he picked up a fridge and ran with it for 200
yards through the forest. Hazard could relate to that.

## A DEATH IN THE FAMILY

When her father died Hazard walked her to the bus depot. He carried her suitcase. She was going home to a funeral. Months before she had shown Hazard a photograph. This is my father she said. It was a picture of a man in a long coat who simply seemed to be walking away. She and Hazard were in bed one night when the phone rang. Hazard heard her quietly talking on the phone. When she returned to bed she said my father is dead. But she said this in a very odd way, as if she had known this already, as if she had carried this information within herself for years. She boarded the bus. Hazard couldn't quite make out her face through the smoked glass window.

## THE MEANING OF SUFFERING

Hazard was looking in a mirror. He looked closely at his eyes. By using both hands he pulled the flesh back from around his left eye which made his eyeball appear big and white. He was looking for lines. A woman he had met had told him there were lines in his eyes that indicated certain health problems which she would look up in her health book. They were seated on a restaurant balcony then. Hazard was talking about suffering. He said a way to give suffering meaning was to suffer bravely. The woman looked in his eyes and said she didn't want to talk about suffering. She didn't want to talk about that. Hazard felt rejected then, embarrassed. He dropped his spoon. Under the table all he could see were her sandalled feet.

## THE RACE TRACK

Out in the hallway three men were racing little
electric cars. Hazard could hear them. He heard the
men shout. He heard the little electric cars go
whizzing past his door. Go you bastard go, one of
the men cried out. It was evident now that the men
were gambling. Hazard wanted to go down and get
his mail. Was the world really this absurd? he
wondered. Hazard walked out into the hall. He
locked his door. A little electric car whizzed between
his feet.

## A THOUSAND SWALLOWS

Hazard really liked her. They were in the truck. She
was driving as usual in her sandalled feet. Hazard
loved the way she operated the clutch and brakes in
her sandalled feet. They were always happy in the
truck. They always had a laugh in the truck. Hazard
had some poems. I'm going to read some poems he
said. Loonsong and thunder, speckled rain upon my
wings. This was just a short one. Hazard wrote short
poems about birds. I am a thousand swallows
flying a bridge.

## THE GARDEN

The woman upstairs was having a fit again. Hazard
could hear her. He could hear her stamping her feet
and her tiny yelps. Hazard had seen her in the
stairway often and she was so small and quiet. Once
Hazard was in the basement doing his laundry
when she came in and asked him what he did. It was
the only time Hazard ever heard her speak. And she
kept this little garden on the sunny side of the block.
Right downtown she kept this little garden with
tiger-lilies and daisies and hollyhocks.

## A TOTAL ECLIPSE OF THE SUN

It was all just a matter of transcendence Hazard
thought as the wild bird swam through the moon's
reflection. A kind of divine pain drove the world but
the pain in itself didn't amount to much. It was
simply something to be overcome, something to be
jumped, like a hurdle. Hazard had seen an eclipse
once. A total eclipse of the sun. The sheer precision
and harmony of that event, at its peak, had actually
driven Hazard to his knees. He was in a back lane
that morning, on his knees, looking at the universe
through a sheet of x-ray film. All the birds thought it
was night.

# Epigraph Acknowledgements

The epigraphs in this book are from the following sources:

page ix:  C.G. Jung, quoted by May Sarton in *Journal of a Solitude* (1973)

page 1:  David Helwig, "Voyage with Brendan," *Atlantic Crossings* (c. 1974)

page 19:  W.H. Auden, "In Memory of W.B. Yeats" (1940)

page 55:  Paulette Jiles, *Waterloo Express* (1973)

page 71:  Boethius, *The Consolation of Philosophy* (c. 522-524 A.D.)